R   ers

S–T	18
U–W	20
X–Z	22
Glossary	24

Who on earth breaks records?

For some people trying to break records is part of their job. Top athletes try to break a record every time they compete. Other people have hobbies that they practise over and over, hoping they can break a record.

Record-breaking attempts are being made every day. Sometimes people **succeed**, sometimes they fail. Some people pick a really difficult record to beat. Other people just like breaking records for doing fun things.

Some people try to break silly records, such as seeing how much ice cream they can eat in a minute.

Now let's work our way through an A–Z of amazing record breakers …

3

Antarctic crossing

Who:	Sir Ranulph Fiennes and Dr Mike Stroud
When:	November, 1992–February, 1993
Where:	**Antarctica**
Details:	They walked 2173 kilometres (1350 miles) in 90 days across snow and ice. They were the first people to walk alone across Antarctica – the coldest and windiest place on earth. No one brought them extra food or gave them help along the way.

Ballooning

Who:	Steve Fossett
When:	July, 2002
Where:	From Northam, Western Australia
Details:	Steve broke the record for the shortest time taken to fly a hot-air balloon around the world (320 hours and 33 minutes). It was also the first world record for a solo flight around the world.

Cycling

Who:	Mark Beaumont from Scotland
When:	February, 2008
Where:	Starting point – Paris, France
Details:	Mark cycled 28 968 kilometres (18 000 miles) around the world. It took him a whole year to plan and 194 days and 17 hours to reach the finish line. He had a special padded saddle made for the trip!

D Domino toppling

Who:	A team of 85 domino builders from 12 countries
When:	Domino Day, every year
Where:	Leeuwarden, The Netherlands
Details:	Domino Day is a world record domino **toppling** event held every year. People try to set up as many dominos as they can, then topple them over! In 2008, 4 345 027 dominoes were toppled. It took 2 hours for all of them to fall. The longest domino spiral was 200 metres long!

Elephant lifting

WEIGHT 969
APPARATUS 105
TOTAL 1074

FEB 21 2007

Who: Sri Chinmoy from India (He was 75 years old at the time.)
When: February, 2007
Where: Northern Thailand
Details: Sri stood under a wooden and steel **platform** with a baby elephant on top. He lifted the platform with his shoulders. The elephant and platform weighed 356 kilograms – that's the weight of about 14 8-year-old school children. It was the heaviest elephant ever lifted.

Freediving
(diving underwater without an **oxygen** tank)

Who: Natalia Molchanova from Russia
When: September, 2009
Where: Egypt
Details: Natalia became the first woman to freedive to a depth of 100 metres in one breath. She was underwater for 3 minutes and 50 seconds. This was Natalia's 25th world record!

Go-karting

Who:	Russell Crowe, Joe Flay, Simon Rudd and Tom Huxtable from Kent, UK
When:	September, 2007
Where:	Teesside, England
Details:	The team of four drivers had always wanted to break the record to see how far a go-kart could be driven in 24 hours. They drove 2056 kilometres (1277 miles), breaking the old record by 347 kilometres (216 miles).

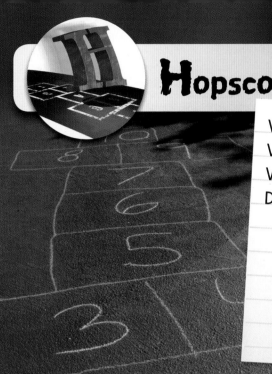

Hopscotching

Who: Ashrita Furman from USA
When: March, 1998
Where: Cancun, Mexico
Details: Ashrita managed to play a record 434 games of hopscotch in 24 hours! Ashrita has broken many other world records – why not look them up on the Internet?

Igloo building

Who: A team of 72 **volunteers** made up of scientists and engineers
When: February, 2008
Where: Grand Falls, Canada
Details: They used 2000 blocks of ice to build the igloo. It had a diameter of 7.9 metres and was 4.2 metres high. When it was finished, 200 people could fit inside it. It was the biggest igloo ever built.

Jelly eating with chopsticks

Who:	Kathryn Ratcliffe from Newcastle, UK (She was 18 years old at the time.)
When:	September, 2007
Where:	A television studio in London, UK
Details:	Eating jelly with chopsticks is much more difficult than eating it with a spoon. Kathryn ate 210 grams of jelly in one minute. That's about as much jelly as you could fit in a jam jar.

Kite flying

Who:	750 volunteers
When:	August, 2008
Where:	St Peter-Ording, Germany
Details:	The volunteers flew their kites on the beach. A judge counted 710 kites in the air at once – a new record!

Leapfrogging

Who:	Andy Wiltz from Kansas, USA (He was 18 years old at the time.)
When:	July, 2000
Where:	Seaman High School, Kansas, USA
Details:	At a school talent show Andy leapfrogged over ten friends who were standing upright in a line! It was the greatest recorded leapfrog distance.

Mountaineering

Who: Reinhold Messner
When: May, 1978
Where: Mount Everest, Nepal
Details: Mount Everest is so high that the air at the top is very thin. Most climbers use oxygen masks to help them breathe. Reinhold Messner was the first person to climb Mount Everest without one.

Reinhold Messner was born in Italy in 1944. He climbed his first mountain with his dad when he was five years old. By the time he was 20 he was one of the best climbers in Europe. In 1986, he became the first person to have reached the top of all 14 of the world's highest peaks. He is known as the best mountaineer of all time.

Number memorizing

Who:	Ben Pridmore from Derby, UK
When:	August, 2007
Where:	The world memory championships, Manama, Bahrain
Details:	Ben **memorized** a record-breaking 4140 numbers in 30 minutes. In 2008, he became the world memory champion.

Ocean swimming

Who:	Thomas Gregory from Eltham, UK (He was 11 years old at the time.)
When:	September, 1988
Where:	English Channel
Details:	Thomas loved long-distance swimming. He swam from France to England in 11 hours and 54 minutes. He was the youngest person to swim the channel.

Paper aeroplane flying

Who: Takuo Toda from Japan
When: April, 2009
Where: Hiroshima, Japan
Details: Takuo folded his plane from a single
        sheet of paper. His plane flew for
        27.9 seconds, which made it the
        longest paper aeroplane flight.
        He had been trying to break the
        record for 11 years. The paper plane
        was only 10 centimetres long.

Quad biking

Graham Hicks has been blind and deaf since he was very young. He rides a quad bike with a passenger who uses touch signals to help him steer. He has world records for quad biking, jet-skiing and for a **hovercraft** flight. He has raised a lot of money for deaf-blind charities.

Graham

Who: Graham Hicks from Peterborough, UK

When: August, 2004

Where: RAF Wittering, UK

Details: Graham broke the world speed record for a quad bike. He reached a top speed of 214 kilometres (133 miles) per hour.

# Rollercoaster riding

Who:	Richard Rodriguez from New York, USA
When:	August, 2007
Where:	Blackpool Pleasure Beach, UK
Details:	Richard rode a rollercoaster for 401 hours. He was allowed one hour's break for every 12 hours of riding to change clothes and shower. But he had to eat, drink and sleep on the rollercoaster!

Snake bathing

Who: Jackie Bibby from Texas, USA
         (He was 87 years old at the time.)
When: November, 2007
Where: Texas, USA
Details: Jackie's nickname is 'The Texas
         Snake Man'. He sat in a see-through
         bath-tub with 87 rattlesnakes for 45
         minutes. The snakes crawled all over
         him but none bit him!

Tiddlywinking

Who: Ralf Laue from Germany
When: September, 2005
Where: Leipzig, Germany
Details: Ralf loves breaking records. He holds records for pancake tossing, domino stacking and tiddlywinking. This record was for flicking a tiddlywink nonstop for the longest distance. Ralf covered 4.255 kilometres. He had a very sore back at the end of the record!

 Underwater ironing

Who: 128 British scuba divers
When: January, 2009
Where: Chepstow, UK
Details: The divers took their irons and
        ironing boards to the bottom
        of a flooded **quarry**. 86 divers
        managed to do their ironing at
        the same time. The record attempt
        raised money for the Royal National Lifeboat Institution.
        Most of the ironing came out creased!

 Volleyballing

Who: A university team from The
        Netherlands
When: December, 2008
Where: Amsterdam, The Netherlands
Details: The players kept their game
        going for 60 hours! They broke
        the record for the longest
        volleyball game ever played.

Worm charming

Who: Sophie Smith and her father Matt Smith, from Cheshire, UK (Sophie was 10 years old at the time.)

When: June, 2009

Where: The World Worm **Charming** Championships, Cheshire, UK

Details: Worms can be charmed out of the ground by making **vibrations** on the surface of the earth. Some worm charmers tap dance, some play instruments, some just stamp their feet. Sophie used a garden fork to tap the ground and created a new world record of charming 567 worms!

X-raying

Who: A team of scientists
When: April, 2009
Where: Stanford University, USA
Details: Scientists have built a mile-long X-ray machine.
It is the world's most powerful X-ray machine. The rays from the machine are so bright that, not only can they show bones, they can show tiny **atoms!**

Yachting

Who: Michael Perham from Hertfordshire, UK
When: November, 2008–August, 2009
Where: The oceans of the world
Details: Aged 14, Mike became the youngest person to sail alone across the Atlantic Ocean. At the age of 17 he became the youngest person to sail solo around the world.

Z Zorbing

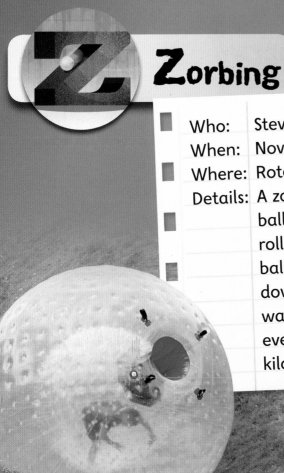

Who: Steve Camp from New Zealand
When: November, 2006
Where: Rotorua, New Zealand
Details: A zorb ball is a giant, clear plastic ball that you climb inside and roll around in. Steve took his zorb ball to the top of a hill and rolled down the hill for 570 metres. It was the longest zorb-ball roll ever and he rolled at around 48 kilometres (30 miles) per hour.

By the time you read this book, some of the records in it might have been beaten. You can look on the Internet to keep up to date with the latest records.

Glossary

Antarctica	the very cold sea and land in the south of the world
atom	one of the very tiny things that everything is made up of
charming	to put a spell on something to make it do what you want
hovercraft	a craft that travels just above the surface of land or water
memorize	learn by heart
oxygen	a gas in the air that everyone needs to breathe in order to stay alive
platform	a flat surface above the level of the ground
quarry	a place where stone is cut out of the ground
succeed	to do or get what you want
topple	to make something fall
vibration	a feeling as if something is moving in all directions at the same time
volunteers	people who offer to do something